please take care of this book

the parable of topsy

by suzanne j. cairns

First published in the United Kingdom in 2015 by
The Choir Press

ISBN 978-1-909300-85-9

Out beyond ideas of
wrongdoing and rightdoing
there is a field -
I'll meet you there.

Rumi

for topsy

please take care of this book

acknowledgements

with thanks to Barty, Baydon, Brenda, Claire, Faye, Frank, Gill, Heather, Jo, Margaret, Nick, Ruth & Pat for propping up this book in extraordinary circumstances x.

contents

taking care of books

a note from the author -

Like all sayings that have withstood the test of time, the idea that 'everyone has a book in them' is without doubt a universal truth.

Our books are as unique and varied as each of their authors, from heavy tomes with dusty covers, to short, gut wrenching pamphlets, that reflect lives snuffed out before barely beginning. Their plot lines are as numerous as the stars above us and their structure as diverse, although like those celestial luminaries, there are patterns that run through all of our stories that connect us, if we only take the time to look more closely.

When the differences between us are peeled away, the skeleton of every human story rests on just two loadstones, love and fear, two dinosaurs that keep us bonded to our Jurassic ancestors. Often disguised by anger, guilt, sorrow, or any of the spectrum of human emotions, it is these twins that knit us and our stories together.

Each person that comes into our lives brings with them an unfinished novel and then there are those special few whose chapters and words become so engaging, so enthralling, so mesmerising that it becomes impossible to put them down.

Their words wrap us up, merge and compliment our own and develop into a new language that we've never known before. It is these books that change lives. These are the stories that have the power to unleash our greatest joy and creativity and the potential to break us into a thousand tiny fragments. This is when librarians are key.

Find the right custodian for your book and you can be sure that once read it will be returned to their shelf, perhaps with a dog-eared cover and a few key pages marked by a sharp crease in the corner, but no one will be in any doubt that this is a well loved treasure.

suzi j cairns

the beginning

bed springs & heroines-a new book

Kate Silver-tongue is doing a samba on her desk, taking requests,
the Taliban are morris dancing and Tom has gone to the movies with Jerry.
Carol is forecasting endless sun and streaks on Brighton pier, just for fun and
there's a super model in the mirror, with a pin sharp mind and a perfect figure,
charismatic as Judi Dench, a mischievous, liquid truffle wench.
Yes, it's a good news day, for a Rossini kind of arching spine,
as you slip your words around my waist, corralling precious time.
So ... you take me onto your pages,
you take me inside your head,
you take me in every room in the house and
then you fall asleep in my bed.
Your steed's smoking hash in the garden,
your armour's been shed in the hall,
your sword's being kept for the ending,
no need for defending at all.

let me

Let me hold your laughter
like a gem,
your fear like a pearl,
your anger like a thistle,
come and be my girl.
Come and slay some
dragons,
come and forge some streams,
come, but oh come quickly,
cos I'm bursting at the seams.
Bring the timid shy one,
the haughty and the sad,
the flighty and the brave one
and the ever so slightly mad.

Bring the one in crimson,
the one in midnight blue, the emerald and the gold one,
(cos she needs loving too).

Don't forget the silly one,
the frilly one,
the Diva,
the musician with the voice of gold,
the magician and deceiver.

Gather up your little folk
in a tender, gentle fashion,
and don't forget the quiet one,
with her, (not so secret), passion.

soar

A brunette silhouette
against an azure sky,
the hue and cry of gulls
wanting more
and the metronomic putt
of old diesel
guiding you to your podium.
We are ready,
here to applaud,
my wink is your life jacket.
Go topsy … Soar.

hush, slush & brothel creepers

Oozing under my skin,
skin on skin,
scented with love,
you invite yourself in.
Words trickle down my veins
and get cornered,
escaping momentarily in tiny gasps.

Chaining my terror with heavy locks,
you serve plates of promises
with forget me knots.
Bubbles of lilac float in my head
exquisite, complicit,
I am finally safe.

the claim

The world claims me as a tree,
a flower,
a blackbird,
a lady bird,
kissing me with
Spring's sweet breath,
laying with me under a canopy of
twinkling courtesans.
Love grows here.

chuckle

A chuckle half escapes on
a wisp of breath,
a featherlight touch on
a perfect breast.
Plumped cheeks and
a rosy grin,
the darkest of eyes
drawing me in.
This is our time
so stay and be clear,
my smile bathes your worries,
my heart tends your fear.

stepping closer now

It took a little time,
to feel your curves match mine,
took a whole load of dust,
to settle.

Now,
we've got our own soft-play cocoon,
where butterflies, poets, musicians and artists
sway with the popping pulse
of happiness that breathes here.

It took a little time
to feel your curves match mine,
took a whole load of trust,
now, deliciously lit up.

tip-toe

When the starlings fly to their roost
and the night swathes us in
universal truths
listen to the spaces between your beating heart,
let fears subside, collide with my love
and garnish your dreams with possibilities.
You are beautiful,
your soul is on the tip of my tongue.

the middle

rose specs

With a trumpet of farts the rose specs depart,
and the twang of a pant makes it clear,
we're an item.
We're nesting, investing,
planning and playing,
the pages are turning, we like what they're saying.
I sleep on the left, you're on the right
the chandelier swings less often at night,
but it isn't an issue,
the spark is still there,
in the glint in your eye and the smell of your hair.
We're on the same page,
interlocked,
happily ensconced,
we've docked.

does it matter if it isn't new?

There's money in antiques,
queues to sell boots,
mileage in vintage.
There's comfort in a comma, when the world is running wild,
relief in a wrinkle when it's scary.
Trees are reassuring, when daisies seem so fickle,
Autumn more erotic than Spring.
I rest my case.

love has come to this house

Love has come to this house,
with its endless pairs of shoes,
tubes of half squeezed toothpaste and empty coffee cups.
It's twiddling with my settings, readjusting as it scans,
rearranging cupboards and has left muddy footprints on the carpet.
Love is partial to a tannoy but then will hardly speak,
hates a rigid schedule, but then regiments the week.
It's becoming quite alarming that
it's allergic to the shower,
except that is on Sunday's,
when it's bathing for an hour.
Love is reading quietly now
scrunched in its favourite chair,
love can be a pain in the arse but
I'm glad that love is there.

ootpat

question marks

A redundant satnav sits on the shelf,
this road is well travelled, you showed me yourself.
You guided the tour, pronounced all the history,
debunked the myth, unveiled the mystery.
Each pock mark and blemish on every arterial,
each varicose vein, the carbuncle imperial.
Here's the bend in the road, the long upward climb,
the outcrop, the bridge, the valley, the mine.
Each scar has its story, each pimple a tale,
each freckle narrates,
I'm reading braille!
But what is this now that I sense in the dark,
this is new ...
this is scary ...
a question mark?

rubik

Perplexed by the puzzle mutating in my head,
wafts of Malham linger on a tantalising thread.
A tapestry of contrasts, should I cower or protect, flecked
with specks of brilliance and

silence.

The Cove is breathing heavily, feet philander on her skin,
meandering on her arteries, but Clair de lune's within.
The old rock sighs with wisdom, there's nothing to control,
keep the faith, the perfect pitch,
I'll just keep trusting in your soul.

ifs & buts

The world is full,
full to the brim,
of ifs and buts.
They sit in shady corners
knitting tangled thoughts,
choking hopes and dreams with robust seams.
They skulk on grassy paths
on windswept days with the what ifs,
and their questioning quiffs and
mischievous blue suede maybes,
deflating the entranced,
harbingers of doom,
like elephants, they fill the room.

brave new world

There's a brave new world
on the other side of fear,
so bring your shadow with you,
we're getting out of here.
I'm not offering you the universe,
it isn't mine to give,
I'm not asking for your soul,
but there's a different way to live.
So take your time, feel my kiss and
wrap your legs around this bliss.
These are just growing pains.

the faustian pact

There are spaces between joy and pain
that have no name,
that at night, shed light on our secret faces.
Places, where the banter stops, the ribaldry runs dry
where we put up our private umbrellas and
look ourselves in the eye.

the end

slippage

There's an uneasy slippage in the clouds today,
the music's lost it's rhythm and the larks have all got gout,
a dromedary fights for survival on a silken thread,
the dawn chorus has taken to it's bed.
Raisins are all dreaming of a plumper former life, and
the hermit in the valley, dreamt he had a wife.
The piano keys are crimson
the cello's joined the drums,
the fingers are feeling crowded
wanting to be thumbs.

something is
not

right.

Single track
road

utopia

Utopia came to Berkshire, after a week or two in Stoke, caught the flu
in Kathmandu,
and in Glasgow just passed out.
In Carlisle it was different, the water there was soft,
but the frosty air could not compare
to the pout of Lowestoft.
Utopia moved to Hackney, when Liverpool got too wild,
and let's not speak of ten lost weeks, in Birmingham ...
Utopia went on a gap year.
The Orient was disorienting, and India far too hot,
Morocco was just bonkers, there was talk about a cot!
America disappointed and Turkey held hands with Greece
and after Rome , it was a side door home, a onesie and a fleece.
Utopia moved to Basingstoke, after several weeks in Slough,
had a dance in the south of France and lives in Yorkshire now.
Utopia it seems is ficklish.

leaks

You came with your soul
spilling like a sieve,
the tundra thawed,
and you abandoned ship.
Now,
one of us leaks as the other one lives.
Someone call a plumber
this woman's not equipped.

vissi d'arte

Vissi d'arte without a heart,
Is like Wallace without his mutt, a rum old joke without the coke,
Izzard without the heels.
So when you grace a space, with Tosca's face,
don't pretend you were never there.

Why shatter this mirror?

Stroke these goodbyes, blunt their spears,
provide a casket for my tears.
Puccini is listening.

cactus love

Your cactus breath is piercing, there's a frost on the hob,
your verbs primed on the horizon,
with adjectives to lob.
My words are unprepared, ambushed by your speed,
lost soldiers in the undergrowth,
strangled by the weeds.
One went over the top, an eager but fancy noun,
but it ended far too quickly
as you shot the poor sod down.
Others followed one by one, their loyalty made me weep,
one was mentioned in dispatches,
(the one you called a freak).
The kitchen smells of carnage, a scent you've never worn,
the silence says, you're out of here,
It seems your job, is done.

incey wincey

Incey Wincey tiger, someone's greasing up your spout,
they've pulled off your legs, one by one
there's no hope of getting out.
Little Miss Muffett sat eating a crumpet,
the spider beside her unseen,
as she watched Jack and Jill cycle over the hill
on a yellow brick road sort of dream.
All the Kings horses and all the King's men
galloped to rescue poor Wincey,
but there were hold ups at Ealing, where Bo-Peep was grieving
so they went to help her instead.
Incey Wincey tiger, someone's greasing up your spout,
we'll get you some legs for Christmas,
just hang on and remember to shout.

the crime

I fear my crime is to know the cracks,
the spaces inbetween
the shadows and the dreams,
the silent screams and pictures.
I dared to care.
To bother with palavers and sagas that few ever heard.
I stopped.
Observed.
Saw the pain submarining
in your face,
a lonely, fragile, hallowed place,
unclothed the marionette and could not forget,
the sheen of a fretted soul.
Now doing stir and crazy along with Patsy Cline,
scolded for my words, laughter dammed,
living in a no-man's land.

the book with no ending

The sky is black and blue, bruised by the
frantic, flailing pages of a dying book.
A book with no hook on which to hang itself
behind the door,
no shelf, no pipe or slippers,
no cocoa or hot milk.
A tumble-weeding, seeding, confusion of dilution.
Call Marple, Ramotswe, Gordon and Gray,
assemble the chairs,
we need a denouement.
Syllables are melting from over exposure
topsy has stolen her words,
we must find closure

...

…

note the
footprints in the
margins, gaps
that make n o s
en s e, fissures,
cracks and
crevices, no
future perfect
tense.

The spine is close
to snapping now,
hear the binding
strain, needless
wanton disregard,
a machiavellian
game ?

…

...
topsy, slide your
words between
the covers, return
them to their
dance, give the
story meaning,
remember the
romance.
Hold it with
tenderness, lay it
softly on your
shelf,
so it has the
chance,
in this short life,
to be read by
someone else.

ps

HIGHER WHARFEDALE:
The DALE OF ROMANCE.
From Ormscliffe to Cam Fell.
By Edmund Bogg.

Upper Wharfdale - The Dale Of Romance

- by Edmund Bogg -

The mission was to find a book that would perfectly portray the sentiments explored in 'please take care of this book'. Auditioning for the main role took place with all the enthusiasm and pedantry of a Hollywood casting. Friends and family rescued piles of small green books from jumble sales, charity shops and antique fairs, the choice was overwhelming. Finally a very tatty book turned up, perfectly proportioned for the photo shoots and whats more it's elaborately illustrated title read 'Higher Wharfdale – The Dale Of Romance' – job done!

First published in 1914, precisely a century before 'please take care of this book' was conceived, with nearly two hundred illustrations and over three hundred and fifty pages, this book was clearly a huge labour of love by author Edmund Bogg. Exploring his background unearthed the story of an extraordinary man. The owner of an art shop in Leeds and too much of a maverick to be accepted by the Yorkshire Ramblers Association, he and fellow artists and musicians created the Leeds Savage club, a more pastoral pre cursor to the bourgeois Bloomsbury Group. Accounts of their adventures on the Yorkshire Moors are both fascinating and enlightening and Edmund's detailed accounts of the landscape rival the Lakes' Wainwright in their precision and historical perspective. Reviving Bogg's work on the pages of 'please take care of this book' was a delight and perfectly demonstrated the theme of custodianship behind the whole project.

Descendants of Edmund Bogg

In the course of my research into Edmund's work and life it was my great good fortune to unearth his family tree and to be able to communicate with two of his surviving great great grandchildren. I would like to thank Michael Bogg and Peter Grice for their enthusiasm and cooperation in this project and hope that their great great grandfather's name and legacy, both continue and thrive.

the travels of a small book

- into the wilderness -

On 9th September 2014 two of Yorkshire's finest Close Protection Officers volunteered to protect '*please take care of this book*' during it's launch into the British Countryside. Suited and booted in bona fide bodyguard apparel, with ear pieces and radios, their presence on Malham Cove certainly attracted attention. Onlookers soon became aware that the little green book was a treasure, in its own way, and soon became engaged with the whole project.

Tipping their hat to Yorkshireman Edmund Bogg, whose book inspired and featured in '*please take care of this book*' it seemed only fitting that the launch was sited in this compelling Yorkshire beauty spot.

At dusk, when the ramblers and dog walkers had made their way home, a robust pair of Yorkshire hands laid '*please take care of this book*' gently on an outcrop of limestone and walked away. The subsequent travels and adventures of this small tome can be unearthed in the second book in the series, '*please take care of this book too – twelve steps home*'.

suzanne j. cairns

Suzanne J. Cairns has always had a love affair with words. She studied them at university for three years in fact and as all those close to her will testify, she often has far too many. Writing in many guises, in both fiction and non-fiction, she is also seduced by images, having exhibited her paintings, designed interiors and been an accomplice in several building projects. In this tome these strands of creativity collide as she leads us all into the gentle narrative of a burgeoning romance and its tortuous decline. Simplicity and accessibility are key in all of Suzanne's work seeking to communicate gentle, universal truths that bind us all.

She currently lives in the Berkshire Downs, drawing on the beauty of the natural world that surrounds her with a dog called Wellie, a buddhist cat called Garlic and a cast of villagers that inspire her, fascinate her and most importantly, put up with her. In 2012, a culmination of circumstances meant that Suzanne was significantly challenged by ill health. Her inability to walk unaided for two years led to the creation of the '*please take care of this book*' series reflecting on the poignant lessons unearthed during this period.

other books in this series

please take care of this book too
twelve steps home

please take care of this book III
tripping on a rainbow

for further information about this book

www.pleasetakecareofthisbook.com

what they think

Robert Jefferson – Journalism Professor, Temple University Japan, TV News Writer NHK World
What a wonderful book of poetry, Suzi! I love it. The pictures are beautiful! Well done. Thank you for sharing it with me. I truly enjoyed reading your work and will refer back to it often for inspiration!

Cynthia Stamy – Specialist Reader at The Literary Consultancy and author of Marianne Moore and China: Orientalism and a Writing of America
Cairns offers the reader a consistently enchanting and sublime collection of poems and photographs which chart the tender tango of a relationship. Her images, by turns fraught and whimsical, conspire to capture the love and fear, the joy and pain, that inhabit us all. *Please take care of this book* deserves a place on every shelf.

Charles Linden – Anxiety Recovery Expert, Author TV presenter
The philosophy of this book speaks, not only, to the soul, but also to the sense of tradition, sentimentality and ownership that only a printed book can generate. It's ethos is simple – we own nothing, everything is borrowed and it is our job as generators and recorders of social history, to be the custodians of all, be it words, images or more profoundly each other. Everyone needs to read this book . . . it's soul food!

Kieran Daly – English Literature Professor, Tokyo, Japan
Your work is exquisite. Now you must read it aloud and share it around the globe.

LS – School Teacher Dartmouth
A beautifully written and thought provoking book . . .
perhaps a reminder to us all to cherish what is important in life.

MB – Translator & Author, Barcelona, Spain
I liked your book very much – nice images and progression of mood, and the photos were evocative – humorous and at the same time wistful, bleak, even.

DJS – Aeronautical Engineer, Devon
The author's starkly contrasted use of literal photography and evocative poetry provides a fascinating view of the contemporary meld of literature, emotion and life.

RM – IT Administrator, Berkshire
Really enjoyed it! If only we could all protect ourselves with bubble wrap.

MB – Lay Reader, Essex
Suzanne has given us a creative and compassionate look at love and life told with passion and gentle humour, a worthy addition to any shelf.